How Can I Function?

How can I stand on one leg?
Think with half a brain?
Love with half a heart?
That's why I've been struggling so.
Somehow, You'll have to fill the gap, Lord.
Somehow, I know
You'll make me whole.

MENDING is a diary of one widow's thoughts and emotions . . . of the questions she asked and the answers she found . . . of a faith that helped her accept a new life . . . without fear . . . without shame . . . or bitterness.

Mending

DOROTHY HSU

First Published 1979 by
David C. Cook Publishing Company

This printing 2011 by
Master's Books Publishing

Design by Kurt Dietsch

Edited by Janet Hoover Thoma
Inside illustrations by Joe VanSeveren

Copyright 1995 by Dorothy Hsu
282 Chardonnay Lane
Lewis Center, OH 43035-9118

Printed in the United States of America

To Missy and Rachel

*In memory of the beautiful man I called
honey and they called daddy.*

The Beginning

When Min died I was devastated, but not destroyed. I did not face widowhood *alone* . . . because of a decision I had made as a teenager. I had recognized, then, that before a perfect God, I was imperfect; I had faced the unpleasant truth that I was a sinner. The Bible informed me that "all [that included me] have sinned and come short of the glory of God" (Romans 3:23). And because of my sin, a penalty hung over my head. The penalty was death. "For the wages of sin is death" (Romans 6:23). But the rest of that verse provided the solution to my dilemma: "The *gift* of God is eternal life through Jesus Christ our Lord." Incredibly, Christ had died for me. "God commended His love toward us in that, while we were yet sinners, Christ died for us" (Romans 5:8). Again, that included me. But since eternal life was a gift, I had to take it. And so I did. In the small country church where Min and I were later married (and where he is now buried), I prayed a simple but sincere prayer: "I realize I'm a sinner, Lord, and I thank You for dying for me. Come into my life and accept me as Your child." He did. For the Word says that "as many as received Him, to them gave He power to become the children of God, even to them that believe on His name" (John 1:12). And that included me. From that moment I have never been alone . . . and I never will be again.

I'm glad one doesn't need to be in a church to become God's child. Any place will do. You can receive God's gift wherever you are—if you recognize your need. And a good time is right now. For without Jesus Christ, no real mending can begin.

More Than the Flu

I suspected from the beginning it was more
*   than the flu.*
He knew, too, I think.
He thought it was in his brain.

I kept telling myself it couldn't be serious.
The doctor wasn't concerned at all.
But why did I stay awake at night agonizing in
*   prayer?*
Why did I break down and cry on the way to
*   work?*

God knew He was going to take him home.
He was preparing me even then.
If I had known about the coma,
*   the gasping for breath,*
*   the tube in his head leaking blood,*
My heart would have failed me for fear.
But the Lord was gracious.
He led me gently.
Slowly He gave me peace.
He brought me through the struggle till
I could say, "Thy will, Lord."
And then He took him home.

No Cause for Alarm

Can you imagine?
My husband was dying
And the squad thought there was
No cause for alarm.
I can't blame them, though.
They aren't God, and only God knew.

They had come the previous Saturday.
Only Ross, being a fireman,
Convinced the squad to take him that time.
At the emergency room, they thought it was a
Sinus infection.
As I said,
Only God knew.

It was Tuesday when I called the second time.
I found him there on the bed
When we came home from the pool.
Unconscious!
Quickly,
Breathlessly,
I called the rescue squad.
This time they would know.
But by the time they came, he had come
    around.

And Ross wasn't there this time.
"Well, ma'am, we're sorry.
We were here last Saturday, you know.
And this isn't really an emergency."
So they left.
They left me alone.
No, the neighbors were here.
Thank God for neighbors.
Because when he went into the seizure again,
They called.
They insisted the squad come once more.
This time
Finally,
They took him.
They took him away from his daughters,
Who would never see him again.

The Furnace

It's still painful,
Extremely painful,
Remembering how it was
In the hospital.
Driving every day,
Praying all the way
For strength to make it one more time.
I screamed inside as I
Walked past the candy stripers,
The nurses,
The visitors.
"Do you know my husband's dying?"
The words almost seemed obscene.
"My husband's dying. He is literally,
Actually, truly dying."

And I would walk along
One step behind the other
Pretending life was normal.
Surely someone would notice.
Surely someone could see the grief
On my face.
I wanted someone to stop me and say,
"What's wrong, dear? Can I help?"
But no one did.

Not once.
Not till that last week
When Min's cousin Reggie and Suchinda
    came.
What a relief to have Reggie pray in the
Room with Min, for Min.
To have him talk to the doctor.
To give me hope when all hope was gone.
The Lord knew I was reaching the point
Where I couldn't go on.

It's been over a month now, and it's
Still painful.
In fact, I don't dig these feelings
Out very often.
They're almost sacred:
Those private, searing pains that
Only You can understand.
That was the furnace, Lord.
That was You purifying me.
That was You burning up all that
Hay and stubble
In my life and bringing me out
Unscorched.

Needing to Be Loved

He had been my husband for nine years.
And in the hospital he didn't even know me.
Not at first.
He just drifted in and out of
Consciousness.
It wasn't a coma, the nurse said.
I didn't know the difference.
At first I was afraid to talk.
It was all so foreign to me:
The tubes in his arms,
The mask on his face.
But soon I learned.
I began to talk constantly during the half hour
*   allowed me.*
I prayed with him,
Sang to him,
Read Scripture,
Talked about the girls.
Just kept up my one-sided conversation
Until
He responded.
I was ecstatic that night
When it happened.
He opened his eyes
And looked at me

For the first time.
He talked to me,
Answered me,
Smiled.
Unbelievable!
I thought he was almost cured.
He even said, "I love you."
I hugged him,
Kissed him,
Cried.
When I got home I called everybody,
Telling them he was so much better.
Cruel, you say
To raise my hopes that way.
No, the Lord knew
I needed that communication.
Needed to feel loved once more
Before he died.

Believing

I can identify with the man
Who pled for the life of his son,
Trying to obey Your demand:
"All things are possible to him
That believeth," You assured him.
"Lord, I believe,"
The father cried out with tears.
"I believe, but please help my
Unbelief."

I believed You could heal him, Lord.
I never questioned Your ability,
But I questioned Your plan.
How could I really believe
When I didn't know Your will for him?
Did Your plan hinge on my believing?
I can't believe it did.
That father prayed honestly,
"Help thou my unbelief."
And You healed his son.
I prayed honestly,
Earnestly, too,
"Help thou my unbelief."
And You took my husband home.
(Another form of healing, true.)
In the end,

It's entirely in Your hands, Lord.
But I still wonder about those words,
"All things are possible to him
That believeth."
I wonder what they mean.

All that celebration
When Min went home.

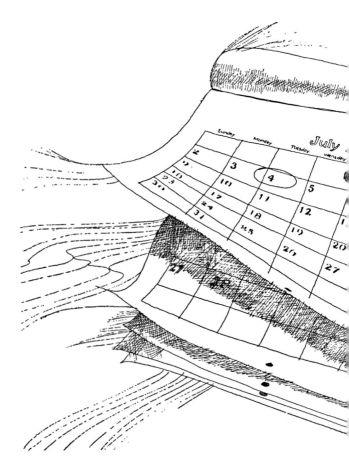

1976

1976
Our bicentennial year.
How many times did I ask him
That in the hospital?
He couldn't remember things,
And I kept asking the date to check.

You see the signs everywhere:
The painted fireplugs,
The parades,
The tacky souvenirs,
And the fireworks, yes,
Especially the fireworks.
That's where we were that night.
That dark, immortal night.

He died at 10:00 (we didn't know then).
The fireworks began soon after.
We watched each one.
The girls were enthralled,
But I nearly bawled,
My heart wasn't there.
It's ironic;
    –No, Lord,
It's appropriate.
All that celebration for our country's birthday.
All that celebration
When Min went home.

Do You Want to See Him?

In the hospital the nurse asked,
"Do you want to see him?"
It didn't take me long to decide.
Yes, I did.
I walked into the room,
That familiar room,
Reverently,
Slowly.

And I was surprised.
Before, during the last hours
He had looked tortured:
Lips cracked and swollen.
The rest I can't describe.
My mind had reeled as I watched
The death struggle
Of my beloved husband.

I had paced the room anxiously
Until I had given in to the final acceptance.
The nurse had said,
"Don't be too strong."
I had laughed.

Actually laughed in that death chamber and
burst out,
"Strong!
Do you know what I've been through?
I've been struggling with the Lord,
And I've finally given in,
Now there's peace."

Now his body was peaceful, too.
I was astonished.
He looked beautiful.
Yes, that's the right word:
Beautiful.
I reached out and touched him.
That gold, cold body that had
Once been warm.
He felt waxy.
I don't know why.
The nurse asked,
"Do you want his ring?"
Want his ring!
Why should I take it off now?
He had worn it every minute.
The nurse said then,
"We must go."

So I left as I had entered.
Reverently,

Slowly.
I didn't even cry.
But I am now,
Remembering how it was.

The Arrow

I put an arrow there
On my calendar.
Pointing up.
July third, it was.
A big arrow that covers the
Whole space,
Except the 3.

I don't really need the
Arrow, though.
There's already one in my heart.

Nothing Stops

You think everything should stop
When your husband dies.
How can the world continue
As though nothing happened?
Trucks rumble by,
The grocery is still open,
Wild music still pours from the radio.
Why?
Don't they know he's dead?
There should be
Silence.
Even nature should pause,
Just for a moment
Out of respect.
But the sun still shines.
The birds still sing.
Not an earth-shattering event
For anybody else but me.
All continues as before.
And for some reason,
I must, too.

Daddy's Dead

How do you say, "Daddy's dead"?
How do you tell your little girls?
It's not something you practice.

I just gathered them round,
Put my arms about them both and said,
"Jesus took daddy home.
Remember when daddy went to
Denver and Boston? Well,
He's taken another trip.
This time he won't come back. . . .
But he's waiting for us."

Rachel sobs.
"How can I sleep tonight,
  since daddy's dead?"
Missy's silent. No response–
  She's older. It strikes her deeper.
  Another day she'll cry.
Simple, isn't it?
To tell your girls that
Daddy's dead.

Just Three

It had been such a hectic month,
That month Min had been in the hospital,
And especially the week following.
The funeral.
The home-going week.
Company was almost constant.
We were never alone.
We needed the support of friends.
Thank You for them, Lord.

But the painful time of parting came.
All left that night but
Grace, Ernie, and See-Yan, who stayed
Till the following day.
Grace and Ernie left first.
See-Yan's plane was later.
He wanted me to go on.
No need to wait three hours at the airport.
But I couldn't.
I knew when he left
It would be just three.
The first time for just three.
The hours passed swiftly,
Like three minutes, really.

Finally, it could not be delayed any longer.
We waved continually as he boarded.
We waved till he disappeared inside.
And then we left.
Just three.
We drove home.
Just three.
We entered the house.
Just three.
For the first time since he died,
Just three,
Just three,
Just three.

*For the first time
since he died,
Just three.*

Bitter

She asked if I were bitter.
We were both in the waiting room
In intensive care.
Her stepfather was dying, too,
Like Min.
She thought I should be, I guess.
She had lost her faith, she said.

I've been thinking about it.
Suppose I were.
I could be angry with God.
I could shake my fist.
I could scream and curse.
I could pollute my little girls'
Minds.
I could make myself and
Everyone else miserable.
Or, I could keep it all inside.
I could seeth and boil
And grumble inwardly
And give myself ulcers.
Either way,
I would destroy myself.

No, I'm not bitter.
I don't always understand my feelings.
They're all jumbled up at times.
But the Lord doesn't ask me to understand.
He just says,
"Let the widows trust in me."
So I just trust,
And let those bitter feelings
Pass by.

Ringing

The phone's been ringing again.
It rang all day,
And yesterday, too.
"I'm sorry about Min," they say.
"Thank you for calling," I say.
"Mama, hang up," the girls say.
They want my attention.
It's all they have now.
Will the ringing never end?
It does, finally.

Then why do I cry,
"I wish someone would call"?

Daddy's Home

"Daddy's home," Rachel cried
When she saw the white car.
He should have been.
It was his normal time to be home
From work.
His car was parked in the
Proper spot.
Yes, Rachel,
Daddy's home.
Forever.

Invitations

Tomorrow at Jack's,
Sunday at Sue's.
I even have to keep a calendar
So I don't get mixed up.
I never had to do that when he was here.
We didn't get invitations then.
Not many, anyway.
But, Lord, we didn't need them then.
Min preferred staying home with us.
In fact,
So many invitations would have upset him.
But now I need them.
I need to spend tomorrow at Jack's
And Sunday at Sue's.
Thank You, Lord, for invitations.

We Always Meant To

We always meant to take a plane trip.
We always meant to buy a bike.
Two bikes, in fact,
With baby carriers on the back.
We always meant to go to Disney World.
We always meant to invite the Chinese couple over.
We always meant to go to Word of Life Camp.
We always meant to.
And now we never will.

One Pillow

"You only need one pillow now, mama."
The words cut through to my soul.
Now that he's gone, the bed seems huge.
Even then it seemed big.
No queen- or king-sized bed for us.
We cuddled up in the space of one.
But some couples share a bed in body only.
They may as well be miles apart.
And some have never shared a bed.
They have their burden, too.
God was good to give me nine years with him.
Nine years with two pillows.
Now I'll be content with one.

The Trapdoor

I didn't know there was a trapdoor
In the bottom of the toaster.
It was Min's before we were married.
I didn't know until today.
I turned it upside down to get the
Waffles out
When I saw it.
Can you imagine the result
When I opened it?
Over nine years' worth of crumbs.
Amazing
The pile it made!
I didn't know how many crumbs
Were in my life either, Lord,
Till the bottom dropped out.
Now I know not to let the crumbs
Collect.
In the toaster,
Or my life.

Fidgety

I was fidgety tonight during church,
Actually restless.
Reminded me of those days
When I was small
And mom had to keep
Tapping me on the head.
I finally decided to write the poem.
Hard to listen
When Pastor Dick expounds
On how to treat
Your wife.

Don't Say

Don't say,
"If you need anything, call."
I need all sorts of things,
But I won't call.
I'm not built that way.
You call me.
Tell me:
"I'll pick up the girls today."
Tell me:
"Bob will be over to mow the lawn."
Tell me:
"I'll help you clean today."
But don't say,
"If you need anything, call."

We would always say,
"Look what daddy did."

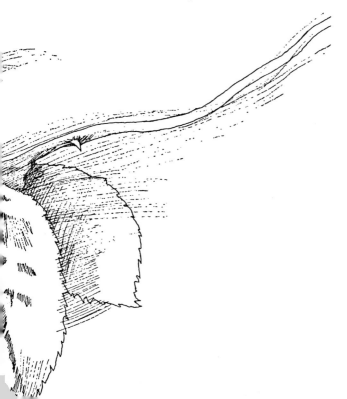

Surprises

He always liked to surprise us,
Since he got up early to go to work,
And we stayed in bed.
He would leave a little sign
That he'd been there.
Sometimes it would be a
Rosebud he had
Picked from the backyard.
He would arrange it perfectly,
Set it in the middle of the table,
And not say a word.
When we girls got up,
We would discover it.
A mute reminder that
We were loved.
One morning a pink, fuzzy bunny
Was peeking out of a flower pot.
Another day a little doll
Was crawling up the cupboard door.
We would always say,
"Look what daddy did."

I guess I shouldn't be surprised
That once more he got up early.
He got there first.
I wonder what surprise
He's planning now.

I'm Glad

I'm glad he got the promotion, Lord.
I'm glad he got the raise.
I'm glad he became a citizen,
And received his colleagues' praise.

I'm glad he finished the basement.
I'm glad he used his saw.
I'm glad he saw the leaves change
On the maple tree last fall.

I'm glad he saw his sister.
I'm glad the girls were grown.
I'm glad he spoke to my folks once more,
Before You took him home.

Not One

I don't find them anymore.
I just picked up the bathroom rug,
And not a single one was
In sight.
I always found so many
When he was alive.
All over the place,
On his clothes,
In the bed,
And in the bathtub.
They almost plugged the drain.
I always loved his black hair
So thick and shiny
My fingers just couldn't keep away.
Although those black hairs fell
Everywhere,
He never worried about going bald.
I had forgotten until
Today when I noticed
There wasn't a single one.
Not a single black hair
Anywhere.

Widow

I didn't know she knew what the word meant.
Had I ever used it in her presence?
She's only five.
It was so new to me, too.
I guess she sensed it was a sinister word
Because she whispered it to me as
We were walking out of the grocery store.
I had to lean over and ask,
"What did you say, Rachel?"
Just three words they were.
Just three words.
"You're a widow."

Why?

Why is it hard to cry sometimes?
It seems so easy for others.
Grandma Combs cries
She cleanses her soul, I think.
Why is it so hard for me?
I want to, you know.
When I sing his favorite hymns
The tears are there.
But they don't fall freely.
For some reason I hold them back.
There's no shame in tears.
Even Jesus wept.
So why,
Why is it so hard for me?

Anniversary

Today's our anniversary.
Last year we visited our special spot.
But this year—
Today's our anniversary.
Two years ago we went out to eat and walked
Hand in hand at the shopping center.
But this year—
Today's our anniversary.
One year we even forgot about it till
Several days late.
But no matter.
Who needs a special day when you are
So much in love?
But what about this year?
I didn't forget this year.
Do you suppose he knew?

Deterioration

Things just keep wearing out:
My carpet's only three years old,
But already
The pathway shows.
My refrigerator was just eight
When it stopped.
Our big tree is already
Showing signs of age.
The car is getting rusty,
And, of course,
Min was only forty-six.
It's just a fact of life.
Things deteriorate here.
Ask any mother.
Pastor Jim said it well,
"We are going from the land of the dying
To the land of the living."
Min just got there first.

Doing Battle

I thought the worst was over.
After all,
Two months have almost passed.
The days seem almost normal.
But tonight, again,
It hit me
With full force.
I was reading a book:
A beautiful book
About dying.
A Christian book
About dying,
When it all came flooding back,
Suddenly, without warning.
A flash flood that left me
Gasping for breath.
Wave after wave
Of overwhelming grief
Threatening to drown me.
I sank to my knees
Beside my bed
Till the sobs subsided,
Till my mind was clear enough
To pray.

It's these moments, Lord,
These desperate moments
When it's just
You and I.
Just us
Facing this struggle together.
What a battle!
Just to keep my chin above water,
Just to keep from going under.
I couldn't face it alone, Lord.
I can't face it alone.

Loving Fully

I sometimes wonder
If I loved him too much.
Perhaps if I had held back
A little.
Perhaps if I hadn't become
So involved.
Perhaps then, the separation
Wouldn't be so traumatic.
Perhaps not,
But then
Those nine years
Wouldn't have been so fulfilling.
I wouldn't have known
Full commitment,
The full experience of love,
The experience of two being completely
One.
Reggie explained it to me,
"The Lord wants us to love fully,
To live life fully,
And when necessary,
To weep fully."
So now I can weep
Because my love is gone.
And I can rejoice
Because I loved.

Words

"Words are inadequate."
How often have I heard that phrase,
Read that phrase,
In the last three months?
How many times have I said it myself?
It's a cop-out.
It justifies saying nothing,
When actually we need to say,
Desperately need to say something.
What's inadequate about
"I'm sorry," or
"I love you," or
"I care"?
What's inadequate about
"You're daily in my prayer"?

Wondering

I wonder sometimes
Would I have done anything different?
If only I had known.
A few things perhaps,
Like fixing breakfast.
He always made his own.

The Attack

At times grief envelopes me slowly
Like a fog
And doesn't lift for hours.
Tonight it came swiftly,
Like a masked bandit,
It attacked without warning
While I walked through a store.
I was nearly toppled by it.
It clutched my throat as I
Walked beside my girls.
Could the clerk sense my agony?
Sometimes I wish I could display a sign:
"Caution–Woman in Grief."
It would explain my actions,
My strange reactions.
But tonight I struggled on with that
Pressure around my neck.
I refused to surrender, and finally it
Dropped off.
I wonder where it's hiding now,
And when it will strike again.

Memory File

Does it seem strange
That I must prepare myself
To remember?
I can't just leap in.
I must wait for the proper
Moment.
Am I strong enough,
Brave enough
To reopen the wound?
Staunchly,
I try.
I probe gently into my
Memory file,
Select a minute,
An hour,
A day,
Relive that time with him,
Endure that bittersweet
Moment of recall
And then deliberately
Slip it back into place.
I'm not free to fling open that
Drawer and reminisce at will.
The onslaught of emotion
Would be too much.

It's a delicate procedure,
This business of remembering.
Safe enough on the surface,
But dredging deeply
Lays my heart bare.
I've labeled the file
Caution:
Handle with care.
And with prayer.

Word of God

Before he died
I read the Bible haphazardly.
Let it fall open here or there.
Instant inspiration, or
Instant boredom.
Sometimes I started a study and stopped.
I could take it or leave it,
And often I left.

But now it's vital.
Now, I breathe it,
Memorize it,
Survive on it.
Why?
When he died my world died.
Everything changed.
But the Bible.
It never changes.

Supply

Calm my spirit, Lord.
I'm frightened.
Suddenly this morning,
I'm frightened.
The toilet leaks.
Winter's near,
He's not here,
And I'm full of fear.
You seem so far away, Lord.
Where are you?
It's black,
So black this morning.
The sun is hiding,
And I'm frightened.
Supply my need, Lord.
You've promised it.
Supply the hope I need this morning.
Supply the warmth.
Supply the light
To brighten my day,
To show me the way.
Let me know that You're near,
Right here beside me,
Right here inside me.

Life and Death

Life without You, Lord,
Is death.
Death with You
Is life.

Content

Content!
What a descriptive word!
Not happy,
Not coping,
Not merely surviving,
But content.
The apostle Paul learned to be content in every
  state.
Can I learn to be content without Min?
Without his touch,
Without his smile,
Without his love.
Yes, I can learn.
The Lord can teach me.
Teach me, Lord.
I want to be content.

Never Again

Why doesn't it get easier?
I've been practicing it for years.
No doubt it was one of my
Very first vocabulary words.
And yet it isn't easier.
In fact, it seems to get
Harder every time.

I said it again today,
And it hurt.
The pain of it kept me awake
During the two-hour drive home.

Of course, saying it to Min
Was the most difficult of all.
He will never say it again.
But I will.
Over,
And over,
And over.

I think it will be heaven's greatest joy:
Never again to say,
"Good-bye."

The Kaleidoscope

I'm a kaleidoscope of moods, Lord.
One moment I'm a composite of
Bright, sunny thoughts:
Pretty,
Precise
Patterns.
I seem to have it all together.

But a quick twist of the mind
Sets those thoughts
Tumbling into disarray.
Suddenly nothing makes sense.
Where has that image gone?
What made me fall apart?

Yesterday the picture soothed my spirit.
Today, it ripped my heart
To see us grouped with him.
The broken bits of feelings
Just keep changing,
Tumbling continually.

What do You see from your end of the
Cylinder, Lord?
Do You see symmetry,

*I can accept
the shifting moods, Lord,
If I know
they're controlled by You.*

A snowflake pattern like in my girl's toy?
Or is it jumbled to You, too?

Twist and turn me till I fall into place.
Till I please Your perfect eye.
Then, hold me steady
Till You choose another view.

I can accept the shifting moods, Lord,
If I know they're controlled by You.

Answered Prayer

Lord,
I prayed for blessing,
For strength,
For courage,
For love,
For power.
I didn't expect You to send
Sickness,
Heartache,
Weakness,
Pain,
And sorrow.
But now that You have,
I'm glad.
Because You've given me
Just what I asked for.

Whole

You said when two marry
They become one.
It's true, I know.
We were one.
But now
My heart is restless.
A constant seeking,
Searching
For something missing:
A churning,
Yearning,
Burning sensation
That's always out of reach.
It just occurred to me what it is.
We were one,
And he's gone,
So that leaves just a half.
How can I function?
How can I stand on one leg?
Think with half a brain?
Love with half a heart?
That's why I've been struggling so.
Somehow, You'll have to fill the gap.
Impossible?
Somehow, I know,
You'll make me whole.

Being Held

There's a security in being held.
To be gently, lovingly
Held by the one you love.
Perhaps it goes back to baby days.
Infants need it.
In fact, without it
They'll die.
I always needed it, too.
I used to ask him sometimes,
"Would you hold me awhile, honey?"
That's all it took
To calm my heart,
To bring that blissful
Feeling of peace:
Peace with him,
With myself,
With my world.
It made everything right.
Just to be held
In those familiar arms.
It's the most bitter cup of all,
To realize I'll never be held
By him again.

Who Am I?

Who am I?
At my age
You would think I'd know.
But for nine years
I lived to please him.
I made the foods he liked,
Went to the places he enjoyed,
Suppressed my own desires many times
To keep harmony in our home.
I don't regret it.
He did the same for me, and
We were happy,
Content,
Fulfilled.
But now, there's no Min to please.
And I'm just beginning to discover
What really pleases me.
What's even more important, Lord,
Is what really pleases You.

Giving Up

I felt like giving up today.
"How much should one be expected
To take?" I railed.
I'm battle-fatigued.
Weary from the struggle.
Day after day
Of pushing ahead,
Battling for every inch.
Keep that chin up!
Don't look back!
Just keep marching!
Fight the depression!
Fight the fear!
Fight the doubt!
Fight the pain!
Fight!
But don't complain.
And when I evaluate my position,
So little ground has been covered.
All that turmoil,
And what do I have to show for it?
A few more wrinkles,
A few less pounds,
Just battle scars.

Why not retreat?
Why not surrender?
Any sane person would just give up.
So I did.
I gave it all to Him.

Imperfection

He wasn't perfect.
He really wasn't.
He left his toenail clippings
On the floor.
He could really be stubborn at times.
And I had to put a Bible verse
Over the steering wheel of his car:
"Bless them which persecute you.
Bless and curse not."
He never cursed, but he
Lost his cool sometimes.
But we adjusted:
He to my imperfections,
And I to his.
We often referred to 1 Peter 4:8:
"Love covers a multitude of sins."
We both had a multitude,
But our love was enough.

Too Late?

I've learned what's important in life.
Too late.
I've learned that snoring
And a sniffling allergic nose are a small matter.
Too late.
I've learned what compassion is.
Too late.
But wait,
Why too late?
Aren't there others who need to know
What's important?
Aren't there others who need compassion?
I've learned just in time.

Separation

"Who shall separate us?"
The verse asks.
Not, who shall separate me,
But us.
That's Min and me.
Nothing can separate us
From God's love.
Not tribulation,
Distress,
Persecution,
Or famine.
No,
Not even death itself,
The ultimate in separation.
But aren't we separated?
Yes, temporarily
From each other.
But not from God's love.
We never shall be.

On Smiles

Sometimes I hate my smile.
Why must it always interfere?
It builds up a wall
Just at those times when
I want the barrier down.
When I smile,
Everyone else smiles,
And then their gates clang shut, too.
Why can't I be honest?
Just once.
Why can't I let the tears flow
And expose my heart?
Why must I always act the stoic
And bear it alone?
You've commanded us
To "rejoice with them that do rejoice,
And weep with them that weep."
Surely someone would weep with me.
Surely someone would,
If only I could.

Just Thinking

I like to think about him
During those quiet moments
When the girls are sleeping,
And I'm not.
I just lie still and think
About his smile,
His voice,
His favorite foods.
Sometimes I can almost hear his accent.

I picture him
As he got up in the morning,
And as he got home at night.
I recapture those moments in his arms,
The moments only he and I knew.

Was he ever really here?
Was he ever really near?
Did I ever really hear his voice?
Sometimes I can't tell.
That's why I spend those quiet moments
Just thinking about him.

How Are You Doing?

"How are you doing?"
They keep on asking.
Can't they see I'm fine?
The girls are fed.
The garbage is out.
And the wash is on the line.

No matter that
My mind is fuzzy
That I long so much to weep
No matter that
The nights keep coming
When I can barely sleep.

Thank you for knowing,
For caring, Lord,
That I'm so often blue.
What a relief
To be myself.
No need to hide from You.

Comparing

Don't compare me with Mrs. Jones
Across the street.
I know her son's in a coma.
And don't tell me to think of Susie.
I know she's got a rotten husband.
I know those people hurt.
But I hurt, too.
And their pain doesn't make
Mine any less.
When I can think clearly,
I'll recognize my blessings.
Right now, the sorrow is too severe.
If you must make a comparison,
Compare me with yourself.
You've got a healthy husband,
A complete family.
You count your own blessings,
And let me discover mine
Myself.

Airport

I had forgotten the feeling
Until tonight.
On the way to the airport
I remembered how
It used to be.
The anticipation of seeing
Him after a week's absence
Was always exhilarating.

As the passengers deplaned,
We would quickly scan every face
Looking for that familiar one
That belonged to us.
"Daddy! Daddy!"
The girls squealed
When they finally saw him.
We all three stormed him at once,
Crowding into his arms
Together.

Waiting for my nieces, tonight
I saw a repeat performance.
Two little girls squealed,
And a daddy enfolded them

While a mother patiently
Waited her turn.

I watched and
Kept inside
My private agony.
I've adjusted to sleeping
Alone, now,
And I've adjusted to driving
Downtown.
But never in a lifetime
Will I adjust to
A daddy coming back.

But never in a lifetime
Will I adjust to
A daddy coming back.

Position

So often
When I have reached the end of my
Resources,
I have moaned,
"I just have to rely on
You, Lord."
As though that were the
Worst possible position.
When actually,
That is the safest,
Most secure,
Most satisfying
One of all.

Talking

I want to talk about him
Just naturally.
While we're talking about the weather,
The children,
The presidential candidates.
I want to talk about him, too.
It's not painful.
It's healing
To talk about daddy.
The girls and I do it all the time,
Naturally,
Without even trying.
So don't think it's awkward.
Let's just talk about him
Whenever.

Depth

There's a depth to my compassion,
My understanding,
My love
That I've never known before.
I shouldn't be surprised.
For I've been in the pit of despair,
And found Him there.
I've passed through the valley with
No one beside me,
And yet, I felt His embrace.
I've searched the deep recesses of my
Heart,
And groped through the dark catacombs
Of grief,
All the while discovering that His
Love is deeper still,
Deeper than my sorrow.
Is it any wonder
That I'm no longer satisfied with
Surface thoughts and feelings?
How can I be content with
Shallow trinkets,
When the treasure lies
In the depths?

Transplant

I see the world with different eyes.
Where was it all before?
It's been there all the time
Just outside my door.
I saw the flowers,
I saw the street,
I saw the mooing cow.
Ordinary, commonplace,
They've not changed, but now
I see Your hand in everything.
I see it in a train.
I see it in the garbage can.
I see it in the rain.
I see it in the teardrop
On my little girl's face.
I see it in the pattern
Of my busy, hurried pace.
I saw before, but now I see
With eyes that aren't my own.
Somehow You transplanted them
When You took my honey home.

The Worst

Imagine the very worst thing
That could happen to you.
The very worst.
The thing you fear the most.
The dreaded harbinger
Of your life.
It happened to me.
So what is there
Left to fear?

Accept It

Do you believe it?
Do you really believe that verse
You've been quoting for years?
"All things work together for good."
You do?
Great!
Then stop pounding on His door.
Stop begging Him to take it away.
Stop the wailing,
And screeching,
And complaining,
And worrying,
And accept it.
That's right.
Just accept it.
Don't try to give that package back.
Does the wrapping frighten you?
Does the rattling inside
Make you shudder?
Just open it.
You may be surprised by
What's inside.

In Him

I was reading the verses last night.
I just couldn't understand.
"Christ in you, the hope of glory."
And "Ye are complete in him."
How can Christ be in me and yet I in Him?
It didn't make sense.

Then the Lord pictured it for me.
A little boat, a wind-tossed vessel,
Floating on the ocean of His love.
Just floating on the surface.
Till the first hole pokes through.
Then the ocean begins to seep inside.

Lord, poke me full of holes.
So I'll sink into You even faster.
Then when I'm low enough
You'll flow over the sides.
Till I'm completely submerged.
Then all of me will be in You.
And all of You will be in me.

Bedtime Thoughts

Little girl's nighttime thoughts are
Delightful.
Thoughts that tend to stay buried
During the day,
But poke their way to the
Surface in the moonlight
And blossom into lovely phrases.
Bedtime's the best time to share those
Special inner feelings.
It's a time when little bodies and minds
Are quiet,
Peaceful,
And receptive.
Just the fertile soil You need to
Plant those thoughts, Lord.
Tonight when I kissed her, Rachel expressed,
From a heart bursting with devotion,
"God's a sweet man."
"Yes, He is," I responded.
"You know how much daddy loved you, and
    God
Is our heavenly Father.
He loves us even more."

She reflected awhile,
And then concluded.
"Now we have two heavenly fathers."
Yes, Lord.
Two fathers still,
And both at the same address.

Since Then

Sitting in the airport
On the last leg of our journey home,
Rachel summarized the trip:
"So far we're all right."
I applied it to our other journey, too,
Our journey since then.
That's how I measure time these days:
Since then.
Since July 3
And so far,
We've been all right.
We've survived a wedding,
Three birthdays,
(All but his have passed now.)
A broken refrigerator,
A balky car,
And now, a plane trip.
Like Paul,
We've been "persecuted, but not forsaken;
Cast down, but not destroyed."
We've remembered him
And wept.
We've remembered him
And laughed.

There have even been some
Bright, buoyant days
Since then,
A few.
Yes, Rachel,
So far, we are all right.
It's a triumph to look back
Over the ordeal and realize
That we actually are
All right.

Togetherness

It's Saturday morning.
Saturday mornings used to be
Carefree.
We could sleep late,
Dawdle awhile,
Talk,
And just relax.
Often we heard
The stampede as the girls
Came pounding down the
Hallway and tumbled into bed with us.
We would all four
Snuggle under the covers.
We giggled,
Tickled,
Wiggled,
Until the girls remembered it
Was cartoon day.
Then up they bounced
As quickly as they had come.
It was a beautiful interval
In the life of a family,
That special Saturday morning
Togetherness

And sometime again,
Either soon or late,
Our family will
Pick up again
Where we left off.
That Saturday interval
Will be an eternity.

Life and Death

Sometimes I feel a twinge of pity
For those who haven't
Experienced it.
I thought I had done it all.
During high-school days
I looked forward to
Getting married.
I experienced that.
Then I yearned for a baby.
I had two of those.
I thought I had experienced it all.
I was ready to settle down
For a long uneventful life,
Looking forward to
Grandchildren,
Vacations,
Retirement together.
A trip to Hong Kong perhaps.
I didn't allow myself to
Think about death.
That could come when
We were both past our prime
And had lived full lives.
Then we could die

Peacefully with children
And grandchildren gathered
Round while we gave
Them our blessing.
Or else we would go together
In the Rapture.
I had never planned my
Life this way.
But now I have experienced it all:
Marriage,
Childbirth,
Death.
And I've discovered that until
You've experienced death,
You haven't experienced life.

Will I Ever Be Loved Again?

As I prepare myself for bed,
Smooth on the rich moisture cream,
Brush my teeth,
Examine my face in the mirror,
A question begins to form:
Will I ever be loved again?
As I dress for church,
Splash on the perfume,
Select a pretty dress,
Try to look my best,
I wonder,
Will I ever be loved again?
I never minded growing old
Then.
He was aging, too.
We loved each other.
So what did it matter?
But now,
There's no man to love,
And as the years take their toll,
As my age begins to show,
That thought begins to grow.

I was surprised to be loved the first time
With my many imperfections.
But now,
The chances seem very slim
That I'll ever be loved again.

Solitude

I shouldn't fear them.
I'm learning not to avoid them.
Beginning to almost enjoy them,
Those desert places,
Those peaceful, pleasant places
Of solitude.
You spent much time alone, Lord.
In the desert,
In the solitary spots.
Time alone with God.
You rose up a
Great while before day
Just to pray.
You had to seek out those
Quiet havens
Away from the crowd.
I no longer need to search for
Time alone.
Suddenly,
It's the pattern of my life.
I'm learning not to dread those
Lonely desert outposts.
We're slowly becoming acquainted,
Solitude and I.
Soon we shall be friends.

Suffering

Who can explain it?
This need for suffering
In our lives?
Before it came,
I feared it.
In fact,
I locked it in the broom
Closet of my mind,
So I wouldn't need to
Deal with it.
I sang with the rest on
Sunday mornings:
"Be still my soul:
The Lord is on thy side,
Bear patiently the cross
Of grief or pain."
I sang
"There's a cross for everyone,
And there's a cross for me."
I wondered occasionally
Why so many hymns
Dealt with trials.
Wouldn't the Lord prevent
Those if I were serving Him?
Weren't tribulations reserved

For those who needed correction,
Chastening?
I wasn't sure that I needed it.

Then it came.
The hammer blows fell
Unmercifully,
It seemed.
Every bone was crushed,
And I lay in a heap
At His feet.
Every dream,
Every hope,
Every plan was shattered.
And I faced a fearful future
Alone.
But strangely,
When I was reduced to shards,
It seems I heard,
"Now, let's build again.
My way."
And He gently collected
The fragments of my life
And fashioned me anew.
The same material,
Yet refined.
Eyes that were tucked away in my heart,
The eyes of my understanding

Have slowly opened.
As they adjust to the light
Flooding in,
I've begun to glimpse the
Purpose of it all,
The beauty of suffering,
The joy of being hammered
Into workable material,
So He can shape me as He pleases.
I still can't explain suffering.
But I've experienced it.
I no longer fear it.
And for it, I say,
"Thank You, Lord."

A Widow

"But I don't want to be a widow,"
She cried.
Her journey has barely started.
I didn't want to be a widow
Either.
But it's like screaming
In the labor room,
"I don't want to have a baby."

The husband's gone,
And like it or not,
I'm a mother,
I'm a widow.
And we make the best
Of the worst.
We're a different breed.

A man doesn't appear in church
For a while,
And we assume he must be dead.
We are no longer shocked
By death and suffering.
We view such as the stuff
Of life.
A new dimension has been added

To our existence.
We've learned to face one day at a time.
To appreciate the
Simple joys and reject the
Nonessentials.
We feel more deeply
And console more effectively.
We face the world with a new
Assurance
Because we have discovered
We are never, ever
Alone.

I fought the idea of
Being a widow, too.
I hated the term.
But now,
I smile.
I look at Phyllis and pray
That the Lord will
Lead her,
Mold her,
Teach her,
Help her one day to pray, too,
"Lord, thank You.
Thank You that I can say
Without fear,

Without shame,
Without bitterness:
I am a widow."

Mother and Father

On my knees
I cried to You, Lord,
"Help!
Please help me.
I'm trying to be both a
Mother and father to my
Girls,
And I can't handle it.
I'm failing."
Kindly,
Gently,
You responded.
"Yes, you're a mother.
But no, you're not a father.
I'm the 'father of the fatherless.'
I'll help you be a mother,
But you let Me be the father."

The Tightrope

It's a tightrope
We widows walk
In our relationships with them,
With men.

We need the male species at times:
To dig us out of snowbanks,
To lift a heavy bed.
We need male advice,
Insight,
Male conversation.
But there it must end.
We're never able to really
Communicate.
Impossible to get really close,
For fear of becoming
Too involved,
Too attached.

On this tightrope, Lord,
We need Your help.
Watch our steps.
Keep our eyes straight ahead.
Help us keep our balance, Lord.

Depression

Depression is

Debilitating, defeating,
Deepening gloom.

Trudging wearily through
The grocery store,
Unable to make a simple choice,
Or to count out correct change.

Surveying an unbelievably messy house,
Piles of laundry,
Work undone, and not being
Able to lift a finger.

Doubting that God cares,
Doubting in my prayers,
Doubting He's even there.

Sitting, staring wild-eyed into space,
Desperately wanting out of the
Human race.

Viewing an empty bed
Two sleeping girls' heads
And screaming,
"Why, why, why,
Is their father dead?"

Seemingly under control,
Until it strikes again.

Peace

Peace is

Staying calm when the car
Conks out at the busy intersection.

Walking slowly, serenely,
When danger is rushing rapidly
At me from behind.

Knowing God knows why the bus is late.
The bus carrying my precious cargo.

Surveying an unbelievably messy house,
Piles of laundry,
Work undone,
And realizing it's not important.

Lovingly gazing at two sleeping girls
And knowing He loves them
Even more than I.

Standing by a new grave,
And knowing it's empty.

Climbing slowly, thoughtfully,
Into bed alone, and being

Able to sleep soundly,
Without a pill.

Most of all,
Walking confidently through life
In His footsteps,
Knowing He is just ahead,
And just behind,
And just beside,
Protecting me.
No need to ever be afraid.

Mending

I've been mending my Bible today,
The one that was his.
So many pages were ripped and
Some had corners missing.
It was a formidable job.
I used "the miracle tape," though,
The kind that doesn't crack
Or yellow with age.
It really is almost invisible.
You've been taping me up, too,
Haven't You, Lord?
My heart was completely torn in two.
You're patching it up with your
Special miracle tape.
It's invisible,
And it won't crack or yellow with age.
In a few years,
You and I will be the only
Ones who know it's there.

You've been taping me up, too,
Haven't You, Lord?

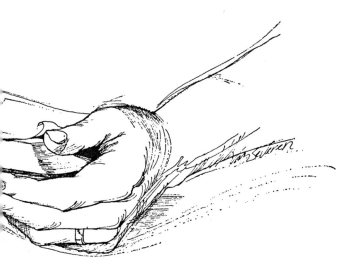

Her Song

She sang it today,
Without any help or coaching from me.
I had taught her the song before.
It seemed appropriate since
Daddy's in heaven now.
"I'm satisfied with just a cottage below"
Was the way it started.
We had sung it in the car.
But today she sang her version.
"I'm satisfied with just a mama below."

A Night Alone

Thank You for a night alone, Lord.
A night to contemplate,
To sort out my thoughts,
To read,
To sweep up crumbs
Without more being scattered.
Lord!
Did You hear what I just said?
Did it shock You?
I shocked myself.
I actually thanked You
For a night alone.
And what's even more surprising,
I really meant it.

Weaving

Grieving is weaving
A tapestry of pain.
The yarn is pure black.
The design sternly plain.
The toil terribly tedious,
No end is in sight.
Work begins in the morning,
Goes on through the night.
Each weaves alone on
His personal shroud.
Locked in the closet
Away from the crowd.
When finally completed,
It's tucked safely away
To be occasionally pulled out
On a dark dreary day.

The Scab

A scab is beginning to form
Over the wound.
It doesn't hurt continually
Like it did at the start.
The throbbing pain
Controlled my life then.
So gingerly I walked through the
House,
Drove to work, and went about my
Business,
Almost in slow motion, it seemed,
So as not to aggravate the torn
Place.

Today we ate lunch together,
My friends and I.
We talked and laughed so naturally
That for the moment
I forgot,
Actually forgot, that I was a
Widow.
Suddenly,
I realized that I am recovering.
Of course it still hurts.
And I must be on guard

To avoid ripping off the scab.
I still can't read his letters,
Or remove my rings,
Or probe my memory
Indiscrimately.
But I know now that healing is
Taking place.
Eventually,
The scab will drop off
Of its own accord,
And I'll just be left with the
Scar.

Lessons

You have a tremendous lesson for me, Lord,
To strike such a tremendous blow,
To exact such a tremendous price.
He was your gift to me,
A precious, priceless gift,
A rare treasure,
His worth far too valuable to measure.
He was the father of my children,
The fulfillment of my girlhood dreams.

I'm indebted to You, Lord,
For such a generous gift.
But he was never mine to keep.
I had to give him back.
And now I'm selfish.
I don't want his death to be wasted.
I want to wring out every ounce of truth,
Every drop of instruction,
And I want to share what I've learned,
To shout it.
I want to proclaim to everyone
That I'll never be the same.
The hard lessons are never easy.
But now I know that the end result
Is tremendous gain.

Home Free

It didn't come suddenly
Like a bolt of lightning.
Just as the night's blackness
Quietly slips away and
Is gradually displaced by
The early morning rays
So that the darkness becomes
Just a memory,
So it was for me.
One day the truth
Finally penetrated my muddled
Hazy thoughts.
I faced myself squarely and
Declared,
"Woman, this is it.
There's no utopia in this life.
That dream you've been chasing
Is just that,
A dream,
An illusion.
Your girls will never be perfect.
Your appliances will never stop breaking.
Your bills will never stop coming.
Your problems will never all be solved,
And your loved ones will never

Stop dying.
That business of living happily ever after
Is still locked in the pages of
Grimm's Fairy Tales."
The truth didn't disillusion me,
Though.
It released me.
It freed me to live in the present,
To face life realistically.
I know I'll suffer heartache today,
Next week,
And next year.
But the beauty is that
Now I know Christ is sufficient
Today,
Next week,
And next year.
And instead of trying to escape
This obstacle course of life,
I face it head on.
I forge ahead with Him.

We shinny up the ropes,
And suffer the burns.
We crawl on our bellies under the
Barbed wire
And get scratched.

We plod through monotonous
Stretches of dry, desolate
Desert.
We stop occasionally,
Survey our progress,
Shake hands, and shout
"Wow!
Look at the hurdles we've crossed!"
Then we plunge in again,
Face the challenge,
Endure the inevitable
Disappointments,
Enjoy each other's company,
All along the way.
And so it will continue
Until the day we finish the course
And are home free.

Adjustment

Last summer I sat in this spot
By the neighborhood pool
And worried about my husband
Home sick in bed.
I could barely interrupt my thoughts
To watch the girls splashing,
To listen to their babbling.
Four weeks later,
I sat by the pool
Stunned,
Immobilized,
Gripped by the fact that he was gone,
Unable to escape the horror
For even one moment.
This summer,
I sit here again
Watching my girls play,
Reading,
Writing notes,
Planning for school next fall.
Only occasionally
Nursing a pang when
A family walks by,
Or a memory floats through.

If that's adjustment,
To be able to sit nonchalantly by the
Pool again,
To eat again,
To laugh again
Without pretending,
To drive eleven hours to Toronto,
Alone with the girls,
Without panicking,
To read a book entitled
Why Do Christians Suffer?
And discover I think
Of my suffering in the past tense.
To finally,
After twelve months,
Switch my rings from my left hand
To the right.
To accept, at last, the fact
That I'm no longer married.
If adjustment is being able
To live again,
Without being constantly reminded
Of his absence,
Then,
I guess you could say I've adjusted.
But if adjustment means
Never remembering,

And never hurting,
Then I guess you could say
I'll never adjust.

Moving Ahead

At first glance,
It's a dead end: widowhood.
I've been halted,
Stifled,
Sidetracked,
Punished.
I've been set aside to collect
Dust,
To wait until Prince Charming
Comes galloping along,
Whisks me away,
And gets me moving again.

At second glance, however,
It's a broad highway
Of opportunity: widowhood.
I've been offered
A unique place to serve,
To understand,
To console.
I've been released from
The demands of a husband,
Not to mope and feel deprived,
But to use those extra hours
To become intimately acquainted
With the Savior,

To meet the needs of others,
Those who have no one to care,
Or understand.
Whether or not
Prince Charming comes galloping
Along,
I'm moving ahead.
In fact,
He may not be able to
Catch up with me.

One Pillow–One Year

At first
I devoured books on
Widowhood.
Sometimes I read the last chapter
First
Longing to read:
"Now I've adjusted to this
New way of life and the
Ache is gone."
But I never found those words.
I wanted someone to tell me
How long it continues,
The excruciating,
Unexplainable pain.
I wanted reassurance that
There was light at the end of the
Dark, lonely
Tunnel.

A year has passed now.
In retrospect,
It passed very quickly.
As I look back,
I see that there was light

All along my way,
His light.
At times,
Very dim it seemed,
But always enough
For one more step.

And that's all it is,
Taking one step at a time.
If you, too,
Want me to say in the last poem
That it's gone,
The emptiness is gone,
I must disappoint you.
It still lurks occasionally
In the closets,
In the men's department
At Sears,
At the airport,
And in a hundred other
Unexpected places.
I believe it will always be so.
But strange as it may seem,
This last year's journey
Through the unknown
Has been the most rewarding
Spiritual adventure of my life.

I've learned that when
All human support is
Jerked away,
God's hands
Gently, but firmly,
Hold me up.
I've learned that communication with God
Through His word and prayer
Is more vital to my life
Than physical food,
And much more satisfying.
One year without him,
And
One year with Him,
Leaves me with just this to say:
Praise the Lord!